Time Management for Entrepreneurs

How to Stop Procrastinating, Get More Done and Increase Your Productivity While Working from Home

JESSICA MARKS

Contents

Are You Ready For Change?

Congratulations!

As you are reading this, I'm assuming that you're already running your own business or you are very interested in making that leap in the near future.

Many dream about ditching the 9 to 5 grind and going into business for themselves. Not everyone has the confidence to make such a major change, but for those that do, it can mean a new level of freedom that can change one's life significantly.

I know what that freedom feels like because I'm fulfilling a lifelong dream of location independence while currently living in Thailand.

Running my own business from home, or more accurately in my case, from anywhere in the world, has been a massive achievement for me and I want YOU to feel that level of success for yourself as well.

Regardless if your dream is to be able to work from anywhere in the world or to work from your own office chair in your own home so that you can enjoy a higher quality of life with your family, the common theme for ditching the regular J-O-B is similar.

For most people entrepreneurship and working from home means a massive increase in personal freedom.

Having been there myself and also knowing many entrepreneurs and the common issues we all face, I know how critical it can be to get going as fast as you can with a good habit of time management and high productivity. I know how easy it can be for procrastination and poor time management to get the best of us if we aren't prepared.

The Problem

A contributing factor as to why some otherwise passionate entrepreneurs end up going back to the same 9 to 5's they so desperately wanted to get away from in the first place, is the inability to manage one's time effectively. Poor time management skills and consistent procrastination can lead to missed opportunities, profit loss and eventually business failure if one isn't careful.

While most go about taking great care to set up the business side of things, very few take into consideration the pros and cons of working from home. Sometimes the lure of being the master of one's own time overshadows some of the realities associated with working from home.

Office Time vs Home Time

There are a lot more "controls" in place when working in an office or other business environment. For instance, your co-worker's five year old isn't allowed to run, jump and disturb others in the office setting.

If you have young children at home, it can be challenging trying to work while at the same time allowing your children to enjoy their home environment. They don't understand that it's not "play time" all the time because you're home. How do you handle that? How do you schedule time for family and your business?

Too Much Time Can Be A Problem Too

It's ironic. The most popular reasons people decide to work from home are to make more money, to have more time to travel, to spend time with family and to just do the things they've always wanted to do.

Instead, often time becomes something work from home entrepreneurs end up chasing like a carrot on a stick!

Why is that?

Well, when you work for an employer, your time belongs to your employer and they never let you forget it. Your boss decides when you arrive to work, what time you can go to lunch, what must be done by a certain time and when you get to go home.

But when you choose to work for yourself, suddenly you, and you alone, are responsible for how that time is spent. There's no one around telling you when to do this, that and the other. You end up enjoying your freedom so much that before you realize it, you've spent much of the day getting very little done at all.

If you don't learn some time management skills and use them daily, you'll find yourself stressed out and "out" of business!

The Solution

That is where this book comes in! I've put together all of the best methods I know of to help create an environment for massive productivity.

If you're struggling to keep your head above water and your work from home dream has become a nightmare because you can't seem to get anything done, now is NOT the time to feel sorry for yourself and just give up!

I've been where you are right now. I know what it feels like to be overwhelmed and disorganized, but working from home doesn't have to be a nightmare when you have the right strategies and systems in place to keep you on track and focused.

If I could show you some simple but very effective ways to manage your time and increase your productivity would you be interested?

Imagine this:

You no longer spend the majority of your time working and accomplishing very little. Instead, you are able to get things done and in less time than before.

Missing deadlines becomes a thing of the past because you have a new system that makes it almost impossible to miss those important dates.

You lead a less stressful healthier life that allows you to have balance. That means you're able to run your business successfully and still enjoy time with family and friends.

You're able to grow your business because you understand the importance of leveraging time and it has a positive impact on the growth of your business.

Procrastination is no longer a problem and this allows you to boost your productivity like never before!

That's just the tip of the iceberg when it comes to time management issues for work from home entrepreneurs.

Did you know that a cluttered work environment can stop your productivity dead in its tracks?

I'll show you how to stop distractions like email and Facebook from robbing you of valuable time.

If you're having problems finishing tasks each day and still feeling run down, your diet could be ruining your business!

Running your own business, especially from home, has a lot of unique challenges, but if you're ready to put in the effort and be consistent, the strategies you are about to learn will allow you to enjoy the benefits listed above and a lot more.

How To Use This Book

It's not necessary to read this guide in any particular order.

The guide is presented in a logical sequence beginning with what are the three main foundational elements for the process of getting yourself organized.

You can also go straight to the section or sections that you feel you need the most help with.

Each chapter is divided into smaller sub-sections and you can view the Table of Contents to go directly to the sections that interest you the most.

Let's get started!

FOUNDATION #1:
Organizing Your Mental Space

Organizing Your Mental Space

Before you can get a real hold on managing your time for success, you need to take some preliminary steps first. You've made the decision to branch out on your own to start and run your business from home. That presents a lot of challenges.

When you decide to go solo it means taking control of your time. Once the excitement begins to wear off, the reality sets in and you realize you now have to answer to yourself. If you fail to get something done and it ends up costing you money, there's no big corporate entity around to absorb some of the costs.

It's all on you.

That's a lot of pressure! So it's so important to make sure you don't end up self-sabotaging yourself and your business. When the pressure is on, you're more likely to make mistakes that can cause you to waste valuable time which can negatively affect your bottom line. I don't think I have to tell you the mental roller coaster you'll find yourself on when you're uncertain about your finances! It then becomes a battle of your mind to keep it all together.

In this section, we're going to begin with the foundation of gaining clarity about your business and everything that you want to achieve so that when you find yourself getting off track with the time management and production, you have something concrete to go back to.

Clarity Is Key

I know what it's like to feel overwhelmed, especially at the start of your business endeavors.

Regardless of where you are at, if you are feeling that sense of overwhelm, I suggest you set aside some time to really gain some clarity about your business, your hopes for your future, your goals…basically everything that has to do with your reasons for making the decision to go into business for yourself.

Schedule some quiet time that is very specifically set aside for this purpose. Perhaps you can think of it as a little retreat for your business…even if the only one attending is you. You, as CEO, are the key person in your business. Have paper and pencil handy so that you can really get some things on paper that will help you to gain the clarity that you need to succeed.

Let's get started!

Know Your "Why" For Your Business

This may seem like a simple step, but I think it really helps to think about (and write down) all of the reminders as to why you've decided to be in business for yourself. If you've recently left a job you don't like this will be easy for you. Remind yourself of all the reasons you want to make your business work

For many of us, the main reasons have to do with income and time freedom.

Working for yourself can mean that the sky is the limit when it comes to how much money you are able to make. Your income can be a direct correlation to the amount of smart time and effort you put into your business.

This is motivation enough for most people to discover ways to succeed as quickly as possible.

Of course there are other benefits to working for yourself. If you are a parent, a valid reason might be that you want to be able to spend more time at home with your children. Running your own schedule can allow you to have the time flexibility that you never could have had while working for someone else.

List all of your big "whys" for starting your business. Hopefully this exercise will leave you feeling extremely motivated!

Your Vision/Mission Statement

During your clarity session regarding your business, it would be a good idea to start creating a mission statement and vision for your particular business.

Regardless of what stage you are at or what it is that you are doing, you will have more success if you treat it as a business from the very beginning. Crafting a mission statement that describes why your business exists will lay a great foundation for that attitude. Writing the perfect mission and vision statements goes beyond the scope of this book, but a simple search online will bring a lot of information and examples for how to go about this.

Here is an article about writing a good mission statement.
http://www.entrepreneur.com/article/65230

Here is an article about writing a good vision statement.
http://www.businessnewsdaily.com/3882-vision-statement.html

Your Ideal Day

These exercises are all in preparation to get you in the frame of mind for being ready to commit 100% to the success of your business, so no matter how silly the exercise might seem, please do give it a try.

Here, I want you to picture and write out your ideal work day. This may or may not include actually having to be sitting at your desk working away on your computer. Perhaps your ideal work day includes a hammock on a beach somewhere sipping a drink with an umbrella in it. Maybe your ideal day means that you have complete financial freedom to be able to pick and choose the elements of your business that you actually want to work at on a daily basis, passing the other items off to a virtual assistant or multiple employees.

Please do not hold back here…the sky is the limit and this is not the time to stifle your dreams. We want to put everything out there and then when we get to our goal setting section, we will pull in the reigns a bit to set out a realistic plan for moving forward with your dreams.

You have to start somewhere and it is critical to know what it is that you are aiming for.

Your Goals

A big part of getting yourself organized mentally includes knowing where it is you want to go (the vision you have for your business) and then building a concrete plan as to how you will achieve that ultimate aim.

Goal setting is a big part of the success of a business and it will be one of the essential elements moving forward as you really get a handle on good time management and productivity strategies.

Begin by looking forward at least 3-5 years down the road for your business. What are the major goals and milestones that you would like to be hitting? These can be financial goals as well as other goals that show the growth of your business. Your goals should be clear and concise.

Let's use the example of someone who is a writer just beginning their self-publishing process.

An example of some 3 year goals might be:

*to have 8 novels published
*to have 20 short stories published
*to have a FaceBook following of 10,000 fans
*to have 10,000 followers on Twitter
*to have 5,000 email subscribers
*to be making $100,000/year from my writing

And then you would break it down further…

An example of some 1 year goals might be:

*to have 2 novels published
*to have 5 short stories published
*to have a FaceBook following of 3,000 fans
*to have 3,000 followers on Twitter
*to have 1,000 email subscribers
*to be making $20,000/year from my writing

Note that for the 1 year goals in this case, I do not break them down according to 1/3 of the 3 year goals because I believe that there would be a bit of a learning curve in year 1. Once there would be some momentum going (as is often the case with new authors), years 2 and 3 would pick up a lot in terms of learning and production.

And then you would further break those 1 year goals down into quarterly and monthly goals.

Your month 1 goals might look something like this based on our example:

*plot/outline novel #1
*decide on the genre for the short stories and if they will be stand alone or part of a series
*create a Facebook page: follow 10 other pages per wk and make 4-6 posts per week.
*create a Twitter account: follow 10 accounts each day and tweet or schedule at least 1 tweet per day
*research and choose an email service for list building
*open a business bank account and create spreadsheets for tracking business income and expenses

From here, you can plot out weekly goals and then your daily task/to-do list.

Your goals will reflect your own business whether it is something totally independent as is the case of a writer, or a business that is service related. If your business is dependent on clients, your goals would reflect certain milestones regarding new client acquisition and your tasks to get there would reflect the things that you can do to find and recruit new clients for your business.

Have fun with this! This should leave you with a great feeling of clarity and the motivation to go forward on a daily basis to achieve your goals.

Developing The Right Mindset

Have you ever noticed that when your environment is a mess it usually correlates to whatever is going on in your life? It's more common than you may realize. If you're worried about finances, getting more clients, paying the bills and taking care of your family, you're going to have a hard time trying to stay organized.

Step 1

Write down any fears or doubts you have about running your business, family issues etc...

Listen, you've got to be honest with yourself. No sugar coating anything! The whole of this exercise is to "air" out what issues may impede your ability to run your business either now or in the future. When your mind is constantly focusing on "problems" it robs you of time. Instead of taking care of business, you end up wasting time worrying and thinking about all the worst possible outcomes that could possibly happen.

That's a colossal waste of time!

So get your pen and paper and write down those thoughts that get in the way of your ability to be productive. If you're having a hard time trying to come up with things, think of it this way.

What keeps you up at night?

The answers to that question are the fears and doubts you need to start writing down.

Step 2

Now read each one out loud. Often when you verbalize something and hear the sound of your own voice it forces both your conscious and subconscious mind to sit up and take notice. It will be a bit uncomfortable at first but don't skip this part.

Step 3

The majority of stuff that we worry about in our lives can be solved on some level. The key is to focus on the things that you can control and allow yourself to accept what you cannot control, but acknowledge that the problem exists.

Step 4

Take each issue and write a possible solution or possible outcome for each. Write whatever comes to mind even if it seems crazy. When you write without focusing on "getting it right" you allow more thoughts to flow freely. That's when you'll have your "aha moment" and begin to see the possibilities for fixing various issues.

Step 5

Now read your new solutions out loud. Now you're forcing your conscious and subconscious mind to pay attention to this new information. Keep repeating the solutions you've come up with over and over again. The more you hear yourself reciting a better outcome, the sooner you'll begin to believe you can find the answers you need. This means you'll end up spending less time worrying about things you already know you can work out on some level.

In order for this technique to work, you'll need to practice on a regular basis. Each time a new "worry" pops up in your mind, deal with it right then and there! The more you do this, the quicker you can get rid of thoughts that steal valuable time from you throughout your day.

Now let's move on to tackling your work space.

FOUNDATION #2:
Organizing Your Physical Space

The Importance Of Your Organized Work Space

In the last section, we went over the importance of organizing your "head space" for what you are wanting to accomplish with your business.

Here we are going to talk about another important foundational principle to good time management and productivity and that is having a physical work environment that best suits your needs and is pleasant to work in.

It is very difficult to engage in good productivity strategies when your home office is disorganized and cluttered. For many people, a cluttered desk and work space is likely to carry over into a cluttered mind and this is what we do not want.

Contrary to this, there is something about a very organized work space that automatically puts one in the mental zone of being productive and very clear about the tasks that need to happen.

In this section, I'm going to help you to create a friendly productive work environment that I believe will set the tone for your new and improved productive work zone!

Organizing Your Physical Space

You'll accomplish a lot more during your work day if you organize your work area first. Clutter is a huge time stealer. When you have to spend time looking for that important client file, your cell phone and a long list of other things over and over again, you're wasting time. Keeping your work space clean and organized virtually eliminates unnecessary time wasting.

Step 1

Choose an area of your home that will be your own personal work space. Ideally you want to choose a room with a door in the quietest part of your home if possible. If you have children or a small home or apartment this may be more of a challenge. Wherever you choose, it should be off limits to anyone not associated with your business. In other words, it's extremely important to establish and clearly explain to other family members that this is your work zone.

Step 2

Once you've established an area, the next step is to furnish it accordingly. This is really important in terms of time management. Choosing the right desk, chair and even your computer set-up all play a role in helping you to use your time more efficiently. Think about it. When you're comfortable don't you perform better? This is especially true if you've got to focus on a big project of some sort. The last thing you want to have to deal with is a nagging backache from sitting hunched over your desk for hours at a time. Pain can be a major distraction.

So you want to choose furniture that will allow you to work comfortably but not so comfortable that you end up snoozing! Try visiting a few different office supply stores so that you can see different kinds of furniture before you buy. This is especially important when choosing a good chair.

I can't stress the importance of getting a high quality ergonomic chair enough. Yes, they can be a bit expensive, but if you'll be spending several hours a day sitting at your desk, do yourself a favor and buy the best you can afford. Your back will thank you later!

Step 3

Next, you'll want to invest in a good storage system. The easiest way to do this may be to look for pre-built office storage systems. This way you won't have to try and visualize what you may need. The work from home entrepreneur boom has prompted several designers to create home office storage units. You can find home office set ups from the very small home office to large scale offices. One of my favorite places to get great storage at reasonable prices is IKEA. Even if you don't care for IKEA, you can get some great ideas by just looking at some of the room displays they create. It's amazing what they can create with some of the smallest of spaces.

It's a good idea to surround yourself with pictures of family and friends. If you will be meeting clients in your home office, don't go overboard.

Adding motivational quotes and pictures to hang on the wall is also a great idea. Whatever keeps you motivated without distracting you from your work is fine and optimal.

A Word About Being "Too Comfortable"

It's important to have a work environment that is both functional and comfortable, but not too comfy. Make sure you're not creating a "second bedroom" atmosphere to the point that you might find yourself drifting off to sleep.

You need to make sure you're able to work comfortably so that you're able to get work done.

Tips

1. Get The Right Chair

Invest in an ergonomic chair that allows you to sit in a way that doesn't compromise your back.

2. Additional Seating

If you have the space, add a more comfortable chair to sit in when you're taking a break or to reward yourself for completing a project, following up with clients, getting your marketing done etc.

3. Dress Code

Although you're working from home and you could work in your pajamas all day, don't! Consider dressing for work just as you did when you worked your 9 to 5. If you were expected to wear business attire, do the same working from home. There's a psychological reason for doing so. Think of this way…in a corporate environment there is often a dress code in place. Doing so helps to create a "look" and may also reinforce the look of professionalism to clients.

It also puts employees in a certain frame of mind. Wearing a suit or business attire means you're there to take care of business. On the other hand, jeans and a sweatshirt is perceived to be less serious and not quite as professional. Of course there are plenty of corporations without dress codes and stress wearing whatever you want within reason.

The point I'm trying to get across to you is to wear clothing in your home office that means "work time" to you. If that means a suit and tie or a blouse and skirt, then wear it. You would be surprised at how your approach to getting things done changes when you "feel" like you're working in a office environment even if that office is an extra room in your home.

Of course, if you can work and be productive in your PJs or sweats, by all means carry on! This is one of the perks of working from home, right?

First Impressions

If an aspect of your home business involves meeting with clients, this is another thing to consider when it comes to how you want to be perceived. Work attire and presenting the right impression is vital to getting and maintaining clients. Unfortunately, people really do judge a book by its cover. So make sure "your cover" is appropriate.

FOUNDATION #3:
Organizing Your Digital Space

Choosing Your Key Work Tools

We now live in an amazing time where digital management tools will be essential for your business. Never before has it been so easy to be connected across multiple devices and be able to take your work with you on the road at a moment's notice.

Depending on your budget, what you currently have and use and how much you plan on working out of a home office will determine what, if any, additional tech gadgets or programs you want to add to your daily routine.

Main Computer

For many people this will be either a desktop computer or a laptop. If your intention is to have a home office and you are also running some hefty programs, then you are sure to need some type of a home computer set-up. This would seem ideal for businesses that utilize graphics and photography services. You probably would not get what you need from using just your laptop computer in terms of screen size. (However, it is easy enough to have additional monitors set up, if your main computer is a laptop).

If your business tends to be more mobile in nature, then a laptop computer is going to make the most sense for you. Many people who mainly work out of their home choose to ultimately have both a desktop and laptop computer for when they are on the go or working away from home.

Tablet Computers/iPads

These lightweight devices have become very popular lately. It's unlikely that you could run your business off of an iPad or tablet for long periods of time, but for certain types of business, these are perfect for mobile work. You can easily do your research, conduct business calls, check e-mail and even write your latest novel all from your iPad. I would consider this more of a luxury addition, rather than something one would choose over a laptop.

Smartphones

Smartphones have changed the way that many people do business today. You can be connected literally almost anywhere in the world via your smartphone. (Note that you have additional costs or things to consider when traveling overseas, but it many cases this is very easy.)

You can do pretty much anything from your smartphone that you could do with your tablet or iPad plus have your phone line for calls and texting.

Organizing Your Computer Files

You can waste a lot of valuable time looking for client projects, documents, billing, correspondence etc. stored on your computer. It's great having all of that hard drive space on your computer right? That is until you can't find what you're looking for.

Here are some tried and true tips for keeping your computer organized.

Consider Having Two Computers

It doesn't matter if you use a Windows based PC or a Mac, consider having two separate computers. You can have one for work and one for personal use. It will make your life so much easier. Plus, there may also be tax advantages as well so be sure to consult with your accountant.

Keeping your business files on a separate PC is another way to stay focused and manage your time better. Instead of wading through files of family pictures mixed in with spreadsheets for your business, you'll be able to keep track of important files and retrieve them much faster. Also, if you keep sensitive client data on your computer you should absolutely not store that data on a personal use computer.

Keep Files Organized With Libraries on Windows 7 & 8

Have you ever noticed the "libraries" section on your Windows PC? Click your start icon and click on Computer. A window will pop up and on the left side of that window you will see the word LIBRARIES.

Basically you can store different files in your library without moving them from their current location. By default Windows has four libraries.

Documents
Music
Pictures
Video

You can also add your own additional folders as well.

How to Use Libraries

Step 1
Go to Libraries from Windows Explorer (See above to do this). Look for a folder our files that are not included in your libraries already. For example, anything that is currently storied on your desktop. Single click to select that folder or file.

Step 2
When you select the folder or file as in step 1, you should now see an option to "Include in library" in the toolbar (above your file list). Now you can choose one of your libraries from that list. For this example just click "Documents."

That's it!

In that same box you will also see the option to "create new library." You can create separate libraries for different parts of your business. This will save you a lot of time because you won't have to remember where you placed a specific file. Instead, you'll just navigate to the appropriate library folder and click.

Remember, Windows does not move the original folder. Libraries just creates an additional location so you can find files a lot quicker.

You can go here to find out more about libraries and view some videos about the process described above.

http://windows.microsoft.com/en-us/windows7/products/features/libraries

Create A Simple Filing System

If you're not interested in utilizing the Library system on your PC you can also create your own system.

The easiest way to keep your files in order is to do so right from the start. That means sitting down before you launch your business and creating basic folders. Now, if you're already in business and you need a GPS device to navigate through your computer's hard drive you can use this system too. It will take some time to get everything reorganized, but the effort will be well worth it when it comes to your ongoing efficiency.

Step 1

Create categories. These will be your folders. Here are a few examples:

Billing
Client Files
Website
Marketing
Advertising

Step 2

Then open each folder and create additional sub-folders. For example:

Billing > Invoices > Due > Paid

Client Files > Projects > Communications

Website > Web Copy > Graphics > Hosting

Marketing > Online > Print

Advertising > Radio > TV

Get the idea? You're simply creating a different folder for different areas of your business.

The sub-folders in each is a way to quickly find very specific files within the main category.

Step 3

Make it a habit to also place new documents specific to each client or other aspects of your business in the appropriate folder every single time. This way you can avoid wasting time trying to remember where you put a client file or information about your website, for example.

Save To Desktop

You may want to save your category folders directly to your desktop. You will be able to locate files much faster this way.

Organizing Mac Files

The Label function on Macs is easy to use, visually cool and will save you a lot of time.

Step 1

Go to Finder > File > Preferences. From there, click on Labels. Look at the top of the Find Preferences window to find the Labels tab.

Step 2

You will see a list of labels already created by default and named by color. Simply change the color name to something business related in each slot.

So, for example, the label named Red could be changed to Contracts. Of course you can name each whatever makes sense for your business.

Do this for as many or as few as you like.

Step 3

Now open any folder on your MAC you want to place under your Contracts label or whatever you've named it.

Right click on a file in that folder and you will see colored boxes. Since, in my example, we made Red = Contracts, we'll select the red box.

That's it you're done!

Repeat the steps for additional files.

The important thing is that you figure out a filing/labeling system that works for you.

Consistency will be the key!

Syncing And Back-Up

Once you have all of your tools chosen, one of the things that you will be thinking about is how to best transfer your information from one device to another.

There are many programs that can make this a very streamlined process for you and you no longer have to worry about transferring information via hard drive or, even more ancient, on to discs.

Evernote is a program that I love that syncs across all devices - use it to compile all kinds of information that you can have at your fingertips regardless of the device you are on.

Evernote
https://www.evernote.com

Here are a few suggestions for general storage and easy transfer between devices:

Google Drive (to set up your free google account if you do not have one)
https://www.google.com

Dropbox
https://www.dropbox.com

You should also consider "cloud" based backup for your computer files. There are many different plans to choose from. Here are a few suggestions.

Crashplan
http://www.crashplan.com

MozyHome
http://mozy.com/home

Backblaze
http://www.backblaze.com

Jessica Marks

Strategies for Time Management
& Good Organization

How to Get Projects Done Faster

Time management is vital to the success of your business, especially as an entrepreneur. We all deal with things differently so there really isn't a "one size fits all" system offered in this book. Instead, I've decided to include time management strategies that work for the majority.

How To Choose The Best Solution For You

The best way to figure out which of the solutions will work best for you is to simply give each one a try. Be patient with yourself. You're going to be creating a lot of useful new habits. You will most likely find that combining more than one strategy will give you even better results.

The most important thing is to get started.

Choose Your Tools

To begin with, you're going to want to choose your method for planning and creating your to-do list.

There are so many great virtual tools these days and of course if you're someone who just loves to put pen to paper, a good old fashioned daily planner will be perfect for you.

It took me a long time to make the transition from using a physical planner and calendar to using something in a digital format. That's how much I love writing things down and for many, the simple act of physically crossing something off your list means a lot! I did finally make the change because I have a strong commitment to being location independent and this comes with having as little physical gear for my business as possible.

Here I will just tell you what I have used (after much research) and loved myself. You are sure to find plenty of other great apps and online tools by doing some simple searches yourself.

I've used Franklin Covey planners in the past and would highly recommend these systems for people who like to use pen and paper. There are many beautiful binders and planning sheets to choose from.

http://franklinplanner.fcorgp.com/store/

Currently I use 2 main apps on my smartphone for planning purposes.

For my calendar, I use Week Calendar which can sync with your Google calendars.
http://www.weekcal.com

For my main to-do lists, I use (and adore!) an app called 2Do.
http://www.2doapp.com

Make A Schedule

One of the trickier things about being in business for yourself, especially at the beginning, often has to do with keeping a schedule.

It is very easy to relish in your newfound freedom regarding the fact that you can now choose the hours and days that you wish to work. This can definitely be a big trap if you do not have clear intentions about your schedule and the amount of time that you want to devote to the success of your business.

Since you are reading this book about time management, I will assume that you could benefit from some good scheduling.

If nothings else, this can help you to start to develop some really good work habits. If you do not have the intention of working during certain times of day, it can be way too easy to procrastinate…watching TV, cleaning, chatting on the phone or whatever else would fill your normal non-working hours.

I suggest that you begin by getting very clear about the number of hours that you do want to put into your business each week. From here, determine the days of the week that you want to take off, if any at all. For some people, especially starting out, working every day along with some time off every day can yield the most benefits. On the other hand, you might really benefit from a day that is completely free of business tasks. Only you know what that best scenario will be for you.

Until you get this down, I would plan out your work schedule in terms of actual days and hours you will work, in your calendar. It is important that you really commit to your work time as it will be essential to ramp up your productivity.

In the next section, we'll talk about scheduling blocks of time.

Schedule Blocks Of Time

You can decide what hours you want to work during the day. This can largely depend on the type of person you are and whether you prefer mornings or are a night owl.

I am a very early morning person myself and find that I feel the best at 5:00AM, or in some cases even earlier, depending on how much sleep I've gotten. I really can NOT do creative work at night, so I need to adjust my schedule to do tasks that fit with how I am feeling at certain times each day.

I like to look at my schedule in terms of chunking project tasks during certain times of day.

As an example, since I am feeling the most creative (perhaps after my first cup of coffee) in the early morning, I might schedule a first writing session of the day for 6-8AM. In general, I'd get up around 5AM, have some coffee, check e-mail and social media platforms and get myself settled for a 6AM start. This doesn't mean that I would write non-stop for 2 hours. I'd take little breaks to get up out of my chair at least once every hour and I suggest that you do this too.

I would then plan for a work break - some news, breakfast and some exercise.

I would then schedule another block of time while still at my best energy level from around 10-1. During this time I would try to also get some more intense project work done as I know I'll be heading into a bit of an energy slump (my pattern) soon.

I tend to have lunch and then a bit of a rest/siesta right after.

My ideal afternoon would have another good chunk of time to cross things off my to-do list.

After dinner, I'm more likely to have something playing on TV (a guilty pleasure) and during this time I can work on more technical tasks or items that don't require a lot of mental energy or creativity from me.

This is just an example of how I structure many of my days. You will design a schedule that works the best for you and adjust accordingly.

The main point that I am making here is that it might be the most beneficial to plan in your rest/break periods (because they will happen anyways) and really utilize those work blocks of time to best suit your energy level and the particulars of your business.

If you run a service related business, your schedule might be more dependent on certain times. These are factors that you will have to take into account and perhaps manage the expectations of your clients when it comes to your hours of business.

Create Systems

I am such a believer in creating systems when it comes to running your business. Even if you are the only person currently working in your business, treat this suggestion as if you are about to hire employees.

Constantly be thinking about each set of tasks that you do within your business and how you can best systematize a process. Even if you don't plan on hiring someone for a very long time, if ever, this can really help with streamlining the things that you do on a regularly basis. Ultimately this will lead to better time management and higher levels of productivity.

Create a written manual of procedures for your business, writing out your systems of operation just as you would if you wanted it handed over to a new employee.

Here are some examples of procedures that you could systematize, using our self-published author role as the example.

*how to deal with fan email
*creating a Facebook campaign that is effective
*a procedure for daily interactions on Twitter
*the process of outlining a new novel
*the process of researching for a new novel
*book launch procedure
*procedure for doing a free book promotion

Basically anything that you do regularly can by broken down into a procedure. This will help you to gain clarity yourself and also put you in a very good position if and when you do decide to outsource some of your business tasks.

The Pareto Principle: Finding Your Critical 20%

The Pareto Principle also referred to as "Pareto's Law" or the "80/20 rule" gets its name from Vilfredo Pareto. He was an economist living in Italy in the early part of the 1900's. The 80/20 rule according Pareto concluded that about 20% of the people controlled about 80% of the land in Italy.

It was his way of showing the unfair and lopsided distribution of wealth.

So how does the Pareto Principle help you as an entrepreneur?

Today the 80/20 Rule can be applied quite well to time management. Several best sellers have been written about the 80/20 rule and there are Fortune 500 companies who swear by this theory.

The theory behind the 80/20 rule when it comes to time management is that you should make a point to focus on the 20% of your tasks, projects, products, etc...that will have the most impact on your business. Typically this 20% is what will increase your bottom line and move you forward.

When I was just getting started as an entrepreneur, I would often ask myself the following question when looking at my daily task list.

"What, on this list, is the fastest path to cash?"

This question can really help you to focus on the items that matter most to your business on a daily basis.

How to Use the Pareto Principle In Your Business

Focus the majority of your time, expertise and energy on the most important tasks (That's the 20%.) and you'll not only end up successfully completing your projects, you will also avoid wasting time working on meaningless items that don't offer great impact to your business.

For this example, we'll identify a typical task list for a self-published author.

Write or Revisit Your Goals for the Week

Take a sheet of paper (or look at the list you've already created during your goal setting session) and list your main projects and areas of focus for the week ahead. For a writer who is working on a new book, a good portion of the week will probably be devoted to writing.

Here is an example goal list for a week:
*write 10,000 words on new novel #2
*set up a free promotion for novel #1 (already published)
*research to find a new cover designer
*create new twitter background
*read for pleasure/research within chosen genre
*create an e-mail follow-up sequence
*create a plan for Facebook promotion that is more organized than current

Prioritize Your Day Making the Critical 20% the Priority

Now, let's assume that it is a Monday and we are creating our daily to-do list with the weekly goals in front of us.

In our example, besides the items listed for the week, let's say that you'd like to get your car cleaned, dye your hair (yourself) because it is driving you crazy, return a phone call to your old college friend and schedule a regular check-up appointment with your dentist.

Now you've got a lot of things to prioritize.

Many of us will find ourselves getting totally distracted by the non-business list and never actually get to those highly effective items on the list. In this case your 20% is firstly going to be everything that is focused on getting the novel #2 published. This means that focusing your first and best energy on getting that daily writing count in will ultimately be pushing you forward within your business.

Even the twitter background task and the e-mail follow-up items, should come after your writing session which is likely to create some good momentum for you at the start of your work day.

If you are just getting started with a service type business and acquiring clients is your main focus, your priorities and your 20% are going to be focused on the things you need to do to get those meetings which will lead to contracts and money in your pocket. Those items might be things like sending emails, making cold calls, conducting research to see who you can connect with and attending local networking events. Other business tasks not related to actually getting and servicing the client, will be within your 80%.

Focus on getting the critical tasks done and you'll find that the time it takes to complete important projects often diminishes. You will also find that the quality of your work goes up as well. That's because when you spend the majority of your time working on the parts of your business that are the most important, not only will you get it done faster, but you will have the time to pay closer attention to details.

How to Put Your To-Do List on Steroids!

Judging from the title of this section alone you might be thinking I'm going to suggest some cool software or app for your iPhone. Although there are a ton of productivity programs and apps out there (see my suggestions throughout the book), for now I'm going to ask you to keep it simple.

Keeping and maintaining a to-do list can help you keep up with client services, phone calls, marketing your business, new ideas and just about anything else you can think of to help make running your business from home successful.

Sometimes we can get caught up in the "shiny new object" syndrome. This is when a new product or tool comes out and convinces us that if we buy it suddenly everything will work perfectly. Well if that were true, there wouldn't be yet another new "thing" released literally every other week!

To get the most out of your to-do list, you're going to need a simple notebook that will only be used for writing down what needs to get done. It doesn't need to be anything fancy.

The purpose of going the "old school pen and paper route" has to do with the way we process information. When you write something down, read it and reread it over again, you are more likely to retain the information to memory. When you create a to-do list via some kind of software for example, it doesn't have the same effect on your brain. Have you ever added something to your Google calendar, set a reminder pop-up and then not really remembered even putting that information on the calendar in the first place?

Think about how you feel when you see an electronic reminder pop-up. Do you feel annoyed and either dismiss the reminder or snooze it for another 15 minutes? More than likely it doesn't bother you to turn it off all together but when you have a list of things to do that is written in your own handwriting there is a stronger mind body connection.

There's something really satisfying about taking your pen and drawing a line through a task you've completed. I find it a lot more motivating to move on to the next task just because I like the feeling I get when I cross off another accomplishment in my day!

That's why I believe the act of physically writing your to-do list makes it more likely you'll complete various tasks. We all like the good feelings associated with success. Each item on your list is a small success.

How To Create Your Business To-Do List

Take that simple notebook and divide one page into 4 sections. At the top of each section write the following:

Section 1 - "Things that must be done today" (Here insert a window of time e.g. 1PM- 4PM)
Section 2 - "Things I need to work on"(9AM - 10AM)
Section 3 - "Things I should work on each day" (4PM – 5 PM)
Section 4 - " Notes"

Don't overwhelm yourself with too many tasks. If you are managing your time accordingly, then you won't be overwhelmed. If you do find that you have too many things to do, you need to change the way you're spending your time so that you can spread your projects out throughout the week.

Next, go to each section and write down no more than 3 tasks for each.

Section 1 should be things that require the most time and effort to be completed. They could also be important phone calls or emails that have to be taken care of above all else. You are the only one who can determine what is a "section 1" task as it depends on the type of business you're in and what services or products you provide to clients and customers.

Section 2 tasks are things that you need to work on and will eventually end up as section 1 items on another day.

Section 3 tasks are things that you will need to work on the next day. These should be written at the end of your work day and may include daily tasks. For example, managing your email, marketing and social media management might be considered section 3 types of tasks. The tasks in section 3 should not require a lot of time, as they are tasks you do on a daily basis.

Finally, use the space in section 4 to make notes about any issues you may have had completing a task. This is going to be important later on. After about two weeks of using this system, you can take a look at your notes. Chances are you will begin to see a pattern of something you're doing that is keeping you from getting certain tasks done. Use this information to make adjustments and watch your productivity increase.

Using Sticky Notes - This Still Works!

If you're among the technology challenged, some of those old school methods of time management are still effective. When you really think about it, most of the apps and other software used to help entrepreneurs like yourself are just new and improved techie versions of old methods.

Sticky notes can help you keep track of projects, to do lists, phone calls, emails and just about anything else.

Color

You can find sticky notes in a wide range of colors. I suggest buying one of those multi colored packs. Office supply stores as well as neighborhood drugstores carry sticky notes.

How To Use Sticky Notes For Time Management

Divide your sticky notes into different stacks by color. Each color should be associated with the importance level of the task. So here's an example:

Red = High priority (May have specific due dates)

These are tasks that should be taken care of first.

Orange = Important

The tasks in this color category may be things that need to be done but may not yet be high priority. For example, it's a Monday morning and you need to have a proposal to a prospective new client on Thursday. You still have time to get it done. However, if you still haven't completed the task by Wednesday than you should move this task to the Red – High priority category.

Blue = Ongoing

These are tasks that you do on a regular basis. These might be things like networking, blogging, marketing, advertising etc.

Green = Completed Projects/Tasks

Major projects and other tasks that have been completed each week should be written on the green notes. You'll add to those items at the end of each work week.

Each task should have its own sticky note. You can attach your notes to your wall directly or purchase an inexpensive white board. Every time you complete one of your tasks, remove the appropriate note.

Why Using Sticky Notes Works So Well

When you use sticky notes, you have an instant visual representation of what needs to get done and when. As you complete each task and remove the note you will feel a sense of accomplishment. Placing completed tasks on a green note allows you to see how efficiently you've worked all week.

Sometimes we can get so caught up with trying to get things done that it can be quite motivating to see how much you actually got done during the week.

If, at the end of the week, you notice that there are still red and orange items that you haven't dealt with yet, this would be an indication that you're not managing your time well and adjustments need to be made.

The Benefits of Getting Up an Hour Earlier

How many times have you been faced with some kind of deadline and wished there were more hours in a day? We've all been there. One way to get more time out of a 24 hour day is to add one extra hour.

The way to do that is to simply get up an hour earlier than normal. Of course you're not creating an additional "25th hour" but you are creating an additional one hour to your day. We spend a certain number of hours each day sleeping, working, running errands, socializing, spending time with family, putting out fires and tons of other things that are all a part of daily life.

When you need more time to deal with an area of your life (like an entrepreneurial endeavor), the key to getting that extra time can simply be to get up an hour earlier each day.

So if, for instance, you need more time to work on marketing your business, use that hour to get the most essential tasks done first within that area.

How to Plan Your Extra Hour

Step 1

When you write your daily to-do list, be sure to include a special section on your list and give it a title. You can call it anything you want.

Here are a few ideas:

"My Extra Hour"
"My Power Hour"
"First Things First"

Step 2

Write down what you want to get done during that hour and make sure to only work on those tasks.

Ideally, you should only have one major project to focus on during that hour. It may take more than one hour to complete the specific project, but don't try to work on more than one major thing at a time. Otherwise you'll end up overwhelming yourself.

Step 3

In order for this technique to work, you have to be committed to giving all of your attention to that one project or area of your business. Don't stop to check e-mail if that is not a task needed to get what you're working on done.

Why This Method Works

When you give that hour a specific title like the ones in the example above, you are also giving it a higher level of importance. It's a mental cue to treat that time as special and it increases the likelihood that you will actually complete whatever it is you need to get done.

Plus when you set your alarm to wake up a full hour earlier than usual, you are also sending a message to yourself subconsciously that the project is really important and worth getting up an hour earlier to get it done.

You won't know just how effective this can be until you give it a try. So if you have something that needs more time and attention to detail, consider using this strategy to get it done.

How Limiting Some Conveniences Can Force You To Work More Efficiently

One day while working from home my Internet service stopped working right in the middle of a new book I was working on. After calling my service provider and after wasting time on hold "for the next available customer service agent" for several long minutes, I was really frustrated as I rely a lot on being able to go online to do research and other related tasks. So I gathered up all of my notes and my laptop and headed to my local library which had free WI-FI access and stayed open until 9PM.

I got there around 1:30PM or so and was about to begin working when I noticed a sign stating that they would be closing early due to some maintenance issue that had to be dealt with. Instead of closing at their usual 9PM time, they would be closing at 4PM!

I knew I needed the extra time to work and wasn't prepared to have my "work hours" cut short, but I had no other choice. So I sat down and got to work. I had a deadline to make and made the decision to get it done by 4PM.

The "Aha" Moment

A few hours later I had completed the project with time to spare. It was only 3:30 PM! I was really surprised that I had not only finished what I needed to do but had also gotten it done before the 4PM closing time. Then I noticed something I hadn't when I first arrived. I took another look at the sign and realized that the date was for the previous day! They hadn't gotten around to taking the signs down!

That meant I still had until 9PM to work, but I was already finished. That's when I started to realize something. When I thought I had a very limited window to get something done I was totally focused on getting the work completed. This was a lot different from giving myself a time limit under circumstances where I had control. In other words, if I had been at home with the Internet working, I would have given myself a lot more leeway to get something done because I didn't have to rush. Having to work under the belief that I only had access to the Internet for a few hours versus several hours, forced me to focus on getting the work done a lot quicker.

Not having the convenience of being able to "slack off", made me work a lot more efficiently. I didn't have time to waste, so I had to get it done.

I'm not suggesting that you cancel your Internet service or anything else you use to run your business. What I am suggesting is taking at least one day a week and going to work in an environment that you do not control. You'll also need to make sure you cannot sit there for more than an hour or two.

For example, many coffee shops, restaurants and cafes have free WiFi. Look for the smaller mom and pop kind of businesses that aren't likely to allow you to just sit there all day using their WiFi without spending money there first.

Choose something that usually takes you longer than 45 minutes to an hour to complete. Not because that's how long it takes, but because you'd typically be stopping to do something else or you'd get distracted by phone calls, e-mails or whatever. Make sure it's something that has to be done that day by a certain time.

Then challenge yourself to go somewhere like one of the places mentioned above where you may only have an hour to get your work done. You'll be amazed at how much you can get done when you're "on the clock" so to speak. The normal distractions won't even bother you because you will be in a higher state of "get it done" mode.

This isn't something you have to do all the time but whenever you feel like you're not giving it your all, this can be a good way to boost your productivity and give yourself a mental jolt!

Technology Short Cuts to Help You Get Things Done

In this section, I want to focus specifically on using technology to manage your time. There are a lot of great programs and apps out there to take a look at and you are sure to find something that will suit your needs.

Timers

Simple timers can be used to keep you aware of how much time you're spending on any one task. You can opt to use an old fashioned kitchen timer, stopwatch, timer apps for your smartphone or simple digital countdown timers on your PC or Mac.

Personally I find timers that make loud ticking sounds a bit distracting. I get so paranoid listening to the time go by that I can barely focus on what I'm trying to do! Digital countdown timers work very well and are quiet until the time is up.

Once you decide which timer you want to use, you're going to set a specific amount of time to get whatever it is you're working on completed. The easiest way is to simply jot down how much time you want to allot to each task and reset your timer to that time when you begin to work on a new task.

A simple Google search online will find several options if you want some type of virtual timer for your computer or smartphone.

By default, the iPhone has a nifty countdown timer built into the clock settings. You can also search for additional iPhone or Android apps that you can use for this purpose.

Q10

There is a free program called Q10. If your business requires you to write reports, proposals, sales material, copy writing etc...this neat little program eliminates all "on screen" distractions. All those icons on your desk top, browsers, games and everything else disappears when you launch Q10. Don't worry because nothing gets deleted or moved around on your computer.

When you launch Q10, your PC becomes totally black. Once you begin to type, the only thing you will see are the words that you are typing from your computer's keyboard. There are no distractions from icons or anything else on your PC's desktop. It even has the sound of an old fashioned electric typewriter as you type and the old school sound of an electric carriage return! Pretty cool!

It's amazing how much time this can save you. The level of focus you will experience is nothing short of amazing. You can get your normal screen back by hitting the Ctrl-Q on your computer. This only works on PC's and is very simple to use. It doesn't come with a lot of information as far as use because it is so simple. Just remember to press F1 on your keyboard and a nice little box will pop up with a list of all of the commands you can use.

Q10 has a built in timer you can set to keep yourself focused on whatever you're working on. It also has a built in auto correct feature, spell checker and it can keep track of your progress for you as well.

http://www.baara.com/q10/

BookedIn

BookedIn is a free to very low cost service that allows you to book appointments via your website. Once you open an account you simply fill out some basic information about your business. This includes things like your name, address, phone number, business hours and availability. You'll be given easy instructions on how to embed your BookedIn calendar on your website.

If, for instance, you offer free or paid consultations for your services, new clients can book time based on the times and days you specify in BookedIn. If you charge for consultations, clients or customers can pay via PayPal before they can book an appointment.

Imagine how much time you'll save! You'll receive an email when someone books time with you, so you can prepare accordingly. There is no phone or e-mail tag to take up valuable time.

http://getbookedin.com

Hello Fax/Hello Sign

The more efficiently you can manage your business, the better time management becomes. Online services like Hello Fax/Hello Sign can help you do just that. Instead of spending money on fax machines, toner, paper and eventual repairs, you can have a virtual fax number instead. All of your faxes are sent to you via email. You can also send faxes right from your PC. You can create fax cover sheets as a template too.

Hello Sign is another service by the same company. If your business requires clients to sign contracts, you can send them via email. Electronic signatures are accepted under the US. Federal ESIGN Act. I'm not a lawyer so it's a good idea to check with an attorney who concentrates in contract law to be on the safe side.

Both services offer free and paid versions and both will save you a lot of time overall.

https://www.hellofax.com
https://www.hellosign.com

Virtual Phone numbers

To make sure you control how you're contacted, it's always a good idea to have a separate business number. For some work from home entrepreneurs, it can get a bit expensive. Virtual phone numbers allow you to have a local or toll-free number which you can forward to any phone you want. You can also set up voice mail and schedule all calls to automatically go to your virtual number after hours.

There are several companies out there to choose from, but not all offer the same services. So before you sign up, make sure the one you choose has the features you need. Some virtual phone number companies like Evoice for example, even have phone apps that allow you to call from your personal cell phone. Instead of your cell number showing up on a client's caller ID, your virtual number would show, allowing you to keep your personal number private.

FreedomVoice
http://www.freedomvoice.com

Evoice
http://www.evoice.com

HostedNumbers
http://www.hostednumbers.com

Time Management Apps

There are thousands of productivity apps available for smartphones. Choosing the best one depends on what your own personal needs and preferences might be.

Tips For Choosing The Right App For You

1. Check the features of each app to be sure it has all of the capabilities you're looking for.

2. See how many times an app has been downloaded and then read the reviews. Beware of apps with 5 star ratings and only one or two reviews. Typically these are reviews left by the developer in an attempt to get more people to download their app. Apps with hundreds or thousands of reviews is a much better way to get an idea of how well an app performs.

3. Make sure you read the fine print. Many free apps come with advertising that can be obtrusive and very annoying. Free typically in the app world can come at a price. This could be ads, promotional pop-ups and even privacy issues.

4. Take advantage of free trials. This is a great way to take productivity apps for a test drive before shelling out cash. Make sure it does what it advertises. Use it as you plan to when you purchase it to make sure it's easy to use.

5. Stick with well known app makers whenever possible or those with good track records. Unfortunately, anyone on the planet can make an app and put it up for sale online. In my opinion you have a better chance at getting a high quality app for iPhones than Android. That's because the quality control is a lot higher with Apple. Google allows anyone to submit to the Android marketplace with very little control in terms of quality. That's not to say you can't find quality apps for Android. Just be aware and do your research first.

Apps for smartphones are still in the "wild wild west" mode so you may end up trying out several before you find one that meets your criteria. Another idea is to ask business associates, family and friends if they can recommend a solid time management app.

Time Tracking Apps:

Eternity Time Log
http://www.komorian.com/eternity.html

OfficeTime
http://www.officetime.net

To-Do List Apps:

2Do
http://www.2doapp.com

Wunderlist
https://www.wunderlist.com

Save Time Using Software to Help You Keep Track of Clients

CRM

Zoho.com is a complete CRM or Client Relationship Management system that is based online. You can set up an account and keep track of e-mail correspondence, manage client projects, create documents and even collaborate and make changes as you work on various projects with clients. You can get started for free. There are some components that remain free and others will require a monthly fee if you choose to use those services.

The advantage of using online based CRM systems is convenience. You can access your client information from any PC with an Internet connection.

http://www.zoho.com

Yesware E-mail

If you rely on e-mail a lot to run and acquire new business, Yesware is an easy to use free client tracking software. Basically, you are able to track who views your e-mails and manage the prospecting process as well. To use Yesware you must have a Gmail address. Once you sign up, Yesware will automatically install in the Gmail account of your choice. As of this writing, you can track and send up to 100 emails free per month. If you require more there is a monthly fee.

The advantage of being able to track your prospecting email activity can save you time by giving potential clients a higher priority and following up with them faster.

http://www.yesware.com

Free Office Software

If you're on a budget consider using Google for creating documents, spreadsheets, slide show presentations, calendars and even video conferencing. You must have a Gmail account to access all of the above.

Once you set up your free Google account, you will automatically have access to free cloud hard drive space to store all of your documents. It's called Google Drive. You can then create folders for each client or different areas of your business that you need to keep organized. You can even share documents securely with clients.

Sign up for Google Plus and you can use Google Hang Outs for live video conferencing with clients.

The biggest advantage to using Google products is the ease of use and the fact that the services are free.

The disadvantages have to do with control. Google can decide to discontinue a product or service at anytime. Although they will give you advance notice, it's still something to keep in mind. Also Google is not known for customer service. So if something fails you're pretty much on your own.

You can create a free account and get started with everything Google related here.

http://www.google.com

Open Office

OpenOffice is an office suite similar to Microsoft Office. Everything you can do with MS Office you can also do with Open Office. This software is completely free and was created by Oracle and is now owned and managed by Apache. Both companies are known worldwide and are leaders in their industry. You can open, create and save documents in several different formats including all MS Word extensions.

http://www.openoffice.org

Outsourcing to Leverage Your Time

Sooner or later your business will grow to the point where you're going to need additional help. If you don't have the budget to take on a full time employee, outsourcing can be a tremendous asset when it comes to time management.

Delegating tasks to someone else allows you to spend more time working on the key areas of your business that will help you grow and become more profitable.

How to Get Started

Before you run out looking for someone, you have to sit down and write out exactly what you want an individual to do for you. Trust me, if you don't know the specifics beforehand you are going to waste a lot of time and money.

Get The Details Right First

1. Make a list of the specific duties you want to delegate. It's not enough to just say you want someone to respond to e-mails. If you want someone to respond to support e-mails, for example, then the person you hire needs to have specialized knowledge.

2. Will the person you hire need special skills? If so, what? Things like the ability to read and write fluently in the language of your choice is a top priority. Will they need graphic skills? Accounting background? If they will be engaging in some form of lead generation, do they have a solid background in sales and telemarketing?

3. Ask yourself some questions also. How much can you afford to spend? Are you okay with hiring someone who may be based in another country?

4. You'll also have to train the person that you hire. That might entail creating a SOP manual (Standard Operating Procedures) to make sure that they follow specific steps.

Yes, it can be time consuming to find, hire and eventually outsource various parts of your business. So you want to do so only when you have the time and patience to find the right person and make sure that they are trained properly.

You may be tempted to take short cuts just to hurry up get some extra help, but if you do, you'll run the risk of getting someone who isn't qualified to do the work at an acceptable level. Remember, the person you choose will be representing your business. So make sure you make the effort to find the right individual for the job.

There are a lot of other steps to outsourcing which go way beyond the scope of this book. I would suggest doing a Google search for outsourcing companies as a start.

Here are some of the most popular websites to find individuals available for outsourcing.

http://fiverr.com

https://www.elance.com

https://www.odesk.com

http://www.guru.com

Jedi Mind Trick To Automatically Put You In "Get it Done Now" Mode

This "mind trick" probably won't stop storm troopers from invading your home office, but it will force you to make a decision between getting something done or wasting more time.

Ready?

The next time you find yourself in a position where something should be taken care of now rather than later, here's what I want you to do.

Stop. Take a deep breath and say this out loud:

"Is the choice I'm about to make going to bring me closer to my goal or push me further away?"

Automatically you're going to start mentally questioning yourself and your choice. You will begin to think a little harder about not doing whatever it is that should be taken care of at the time. It forces you to take a look at what you're doing in the moment. When you ask yourself this question your mind starts to think about the longer term ramifications of not doing a specific task and keeping commitments to yourself.

Now, I'm not going to tell you that you're going to opt to go ahead and get whatever it is done every single time. We're all human and we all make poor choices from time to time, but the more you become increasingly conscious of your day to day decisions, the more you will choose the task over other things that just distract from your business goals.

Why?

It's a psychological thing. It's like a little nagging voice inside that almost forces you to be accountable and take care of business or suffer the consequences. In business, the consequences of lost time and money can be great motivators.

Write that sentence down and post it in your home office space where you can see it. The next time you want to do something you know wouldn't be the best choice, read it out loud and see what happens.

Keeping A Calendar To Stay Organized

Using a simple calendar to keep track of daily tasks is another tool to help you manage your time better.

A desk or wall calendar can be great for allowing you to quickly see what's scheduled at a glance while you are working. Consider using colored markers for different categories. Just as I suggested with sticky notes, colors stand out and can bring different things to your attention faster.

Even if you're using a to-do list, a calendar is another way to track and enforce the importance of getting things done. You can make a calendar that is your main system or use it as a back-up. It really depends on what works best for you.

A friend of mine uses the sticky note method I went over in the previous section. She also has a big wall calendar with basically the same information. When she's on a call with a client, she glances at the wall calendar when discussing specific dates and time frames. For her, it works better than rifling through the pages of her to-do lists.

A calendar is also great if you have to make in person visits with clients. Many people prefer a date book with plenty of space for notes that can be carried and used while on the go. You can also use the calendar function on your smartphone if you have one. Although sometimes adding notes from a meeting and inputting it into a smartphone isn't always as easy or practical as simply writing it down. You can always add key notes to your phone later.

There are many different calendar and planner type tools that can suit a wide variety of needs, so it shouldn't be a problem finding something that will work for you and your business.

The Multitasking Myth

The term multitasking has become the go to word for a lot of employers in an attempt to get employees to get more work done. Employers like to throw that word around when they want you to do the job of two or three individuals, because it saves them money not having to pay additional salaries. Or maybe they want something else done in addition to what you already have on your plate, so they tell you to multitask and you'll get it all done!

Tah dah!!!

So it's no wonder that when you begin working from home, it's easy to fall into the trap of thinking you can multitask your way to success. Instead, what ends up happening is that you get overwhelmed with way too much to get done in a short period of time all because you believe you can multitask everything.

Multitasking Isn't What You Think It Is

Let me explain. Multitasking for most people is the ability to do more than one thing at a time. That might mean working on more than one project simultaneously, while still being able to run meetings, errands and a long list other things. The belief is that if you can do a lot of different tasks at the same time, you're multitasking.

The Problem

The problem is that our brains do not have the ability to give 100% of our focus to more than one thing at a time. So, if you are splitting your attention in order to get several things done, I can almost guarantee that you're going to end up making some major mistakes somewhere that may not have been made if you were instead giving your undivided attention to one task at a time. It doesn't matter what it is you're trying to do, the results will be the same.

Here's an example:

In almost every state in the US it is now illegal to drive a car and talk on your cell phone unless you're wearing a headset. The reason is to keep drivers from being distracted on the road. When you're trying to talk to someone and also trying to pay attention while you drive, your brain has to choose which one to give its undivided attention to. Think about it. Have you ever been on your cell phone talking while you were driving and missed an exit that you take every day? Or ran a stop sign or almost had an accident because you didn't realize the car ahead of you had stopped?

I saw a video on the news where a guy was so focused while texting on his phone that he walked off the subway platform! Lucky for him that another person pulled him to safety as a train was just seconds away.

The reason dangerous things like in the above examples happen, is because the brain is trying to "multitask" and do more than one thing at a time but it cannot. We're not wired that way. Recently, researchers announced that wearing a headset while driving doesn't reduce the likelihood of getting into an accident.

Duh!

That's why I say that multitasking by the most common definition is a myth. That's not to say you can't work on more than one thing at a time. You can. Just don't expect your best work to be the end result. You end up getting mentally fatigued and that's when mistakes happen.

So Now What?

My best advice is to plan your work using one or more of the methods I've given you in this book. Planning out time schedules and creating workable plans within a reasonable amount of time is the best way to go.

Try not to take on projects at the last minute or if you have a full schedule already. The lure of making money often makes many entrepreneurs take on too much fearing times when work may be slow.

To keep that from happening, make sure you are always marketing your business. If you have a constant stream of inquiries about your business you won't have to worry about the "feast or famine" syndrome that so many work from home entrepreneurs deal with.

The Best Time of Day To Get The Most Difficult Tasks Done

One of my favorite shows to watch was Fear Factor. You know the show where you could win $50K after doing a series of scary stunts and also usually eating something really gross? Whenever there was a challenge to eat more than one disgusting thing, I noticed many contestants would opt to eat the worse thing first, just to get it out of the way.

Author Brian Tracy wrote a book that is now considered a classic called Eat That Frog. If that makes you squeamish, that's great! It's supposed to, unless of course, you actually like eating frogs! In any case, the point of that book is in my opinion one of the best strategies for getting difficult tasks done. It's the same strategy those contestants used on Fear Factor.

Do the most difficult task first (eat that frog) and the rest of your day is literally a piece of cake! Whatever it is that you most dread doing for the day should go at the very top of your to-do list before everything else. Perhaps it will be your early morning "power hour" item. Then you must actually do the thing on your list!

Why Do The Tough Items First?

How you start your day tends to set the stage for the rest of your day. Raise your hand if you've ever gone to work after not sleeping well and spent the entire day in a bad mood? The same thing can happen if you choose to do the easiest items on your list first. If you start your day doing all of the easy things, you're not going to be too happy knowing in the back of your mind that you still have to deal with that difficult task, project, phone call or whatever it may be. Instead, if you get up and focus on getting that difficult task done, you can go about the rest of your day feeling pretty good about yourself.

It's done and out of the way!

Besides, the later you wait to start on a difficult task the greater the risk of you not doing it at all or not doing the best job you could.

Getting It Done!

Step 1

Take a look at your to-do list and choose one item that you're dreading. It's the one that makes you roll your eyes towards the ceiling every time you think about it!

Step 2

Move it to the top of your list and plan to tackle it as the first thing you do when you start your day. In a previous section, I talked about the benefits of getting up an hour earlier each day. If you haven't read that section please do so as that hour may be the best time for you to eat that frog!

Step 3

Stay consistent and notice how much time you are able to save. Plus when you get the tough stuff out of the way earlier, you're less likely to spend your personal time trying to catch up.

Create A 30 Day Challenge

I am a big believer in making strong commitments to yourself in order to create some massive momentum.

I like to do 30 day challenges whenever I want to experiment or create a new habit for myself. The key is to think of something that over 30 days could really create a positive change within your life. In the context of this book, we are focusing on business productivity.

Think of one thing that you could commit to doing for 30 days without fail and vow to give this your best shot, if nothing else, for the experiment of it all.

Here are some examples,

If you are a writer having a difficult time with the actual "writing" part of your business, (Hey, we've all been there.) perhaps you could challenge yourself to get up 1 hour earlier than normal JUST to dedicate to your writing first thing of the day. If mornings are not a good time for you, choose another challenge that involves making this one hour of writing top priority. Imagine how it would feel at the end of a month having an additional 30 hours of writing to add to your current project?

If you are in a service related business that depends on acquiring new clients, maybe your challenge would be to send x number of e-mails per day and/or make x number of cold calls per day.

Assuming you have an online presence for your business (and you should!), your 30 day challenge might include 30 minutes of promotional activities each day. This could further be identified as social media management or whatever platform you feel would give the greatest impact to your business during this time.

Based on the types of tasks that you feel you "should" be doing for your business, you should have no trouble figuring out which types of things would be the best for you to target within a specific period of time.

Remind yourself of your vision and goals for YOUR business! And good luck!

Tips for Avoiding Time Traps & Overcoming Procrastination

Common Time Traps & How to Avoid Them

If you lined up 100 work from home entrepreneurs and asked them what are some of the biggest issues they face when it comes to managing their time, there's no doubt in my mind that the following issues would all rank pretty high.

There are probably at least 2 or 3 issues you may be having a hard time trying to deal with right now. I will give you a simple strategy to deal with each one and before you know it you'll be sailing through your work day and getting a lot more done with fewer interruptions.

Establish Your Work Hours

Hold yourself accountable for your business by setting real working hours. When you do that you are making it clear to yourself, your family and your clients that you are serious about your business.

Also, having specific working hours will help you to stay focused and get into work mode during that time. This is not to say that you can't be flexible with your time, because, after all, that's one of the reasons you decided to work for yourself.

Right?

But if you're not careful you'll end up not being a master of your time. Instead, you'll end up constantly trying to keep up with various aspects of your business yet never really accomplishing a whole lot. When you work for an employer you're always watching the clock to make sure you reach deadlines, make important phone calls and answer emails before quitting time. You should do the same for your own business.

Do yourself a favor and decide what your regular business hours will be and stick to it. If you're not a morning person, then start your business hours late morning. You can always give clients or customers a "window of time" when they can expect a response to phone calls and emails. You don't have to tell them you don't get up until 10:00AM! Keep that secret to yourself.

Choosing Working Hours

This can be a bit tricky because everyone has a different situation. If you have children who are in school, for example, you may have to adjust your hours around their schedule. In some cases, you may have to start your working hours much earlier in the day. Of course, the kind of business you're in also plays a part in what your hours will be.

Just make sure that you choose a span of time that makes sense for both your business and you. You may have to experiment in the beginning to find something that works best.

Time Is Money!

There's no right or wrong set of hours, but you need to decide when your work day begins and stick to it. Work from home entrepreneurs get so wrapped up in the freedom thing that they end up getting overwhelmed because they haven't established working hours. Working for someone else means you're expected to arrive at work by a certain time every work day. There are several reasons why this is so, but mainly it's so that an employer can track your work time and make sure they are getting a good ROI or return on investment in terms of what they pay you.

You should be doing the same. Keeping track of your time allows you to price your services and bill clients accordingly if you are in a service related business. You also need to be able to have a set amount of work time for various client projects to make sure that you're not working overtime on low paying projects.

If you are a writer, as another example, it is a good idea to track how long your writing projects take you so that you can get an idea of your return on investment for these types of hours also.

If you're willing to do that for someone else, then it should be something you're willing to do for the success of your own business. So make your time count and maintain consistent working hours.

How to Quit Working

It's so important to have an "end of the work day" routine. If you don't, you'll find yourself working more than you're sleeping. The reason this is so important when it comes to time management is simply because if you're over working yourself you may end up getting a lot less sleep. Lack of sleep means that at some point your body will not be operating at optimum levels. Eventually you'll end up catching up on your sleep during what should be working hours. This then can lead to missed deadlines, angry clients and ultimately loss of business and profits.

So it's crucial to create a regular routine that signals to you on a subconscious level that it's time to stop working and rest. You need to be able to refresh your body, your mind and your spirit so that you'll be ready to work the next business day.

Just as you've established the business hours for your business, you need to establish a routine of ending your work day. There are tons of ways to do this and here are a few ideas to get you started in the right direction.

Step 1

About a half an hour before the end of your work day begin cleaning up your work area and preparing for the following day. Make sure you have your to-do list for the next day prepared. If there is something you did not complete, don't work on it if at all possible after working hours. Add it as a priority on your to-do list for the next day.

Step 2

Do not take work to bed with you. Make your bedroom a "no work zone" no matter how tempting it may be. Besides, if you're married or have a significant other, they might not appreciate it if you're always working. Your friends and family deserve some free time with you too. Let after hour business calls go to voice mail and resist checking your e-mail after work hours.

You also need some personal time to unwind and pamper yourself. Thinking about work can interfere with your ability to get a good night of sleep so leave work in your office until the next morning.

Step 3

Make it a habit to lock up your home office just as you would if you were working for someone else. Chances are you wouldn't go back to work at midnight to work on a client file right?

So why do so at home just because you can?

Remember, one of the reasons you've chosen to become a work from home entrepreneur is to enjoy the freedoms that comes along with that choice. So take time to enjoy that freedom.

Make Sure Everyone Else is Aware Of Your Working Hours

It's funny. When you decide to work from home, your family, friends and even clients think "you're not really working" because you're at home! Maybe it's a psychological thing with people. I don't know why it is that people have this perception, but I can't stress how important it is to let the world know that just because you work from home, it doesn't mean you're available to them whenever they want.

How to Enforce Contact Rules With Family & Friends

Keep in mind that you have to control your time when you work from home. If family and friends keep dropping by unannounced or calling just to shoot the breeze, nip it in the bud right from the start.

One way to do this is to explain what your business is about and what is required to be successful. Then let them know that unless there is an emergency you will not be available during your business hours.

Here's an example of what you might say to a friend or family member.

"I work from home as a virtual assistant which means my clients pay me to manage a lot of important details. So in order to make sure I am providing quality service, I have to maintain consistent business hours. I would love to chat with you and hang out but only when I'm not working. My business hours are from 8AM to 4PM Monday through Friday. So unless it's an emergency please call or stop by after 4PM."

I know what you're thinking. "Yeah right...how am I going to enforce those rules?"

It's actually a lot easier than you realize.

Here's how to do it.

Once you've had a conversation like the example above, you can enforce your rules by making sure that you don't break the rules. That means not giving in and sticking to the hours you've established. Here's an example on how to deal with friends and family.

Scenario – A family member or friend calls you during business hours because she's bored and wants to chit-chat.

First, always be polite. Most of the people in your life aren't out to sabotage you. If they do not work from home, they have no idea how difficult time management can be. So in this scenario, ask if this is an emergency. If not, kindly remind your friend that you're working but you'll be happy to talk to her after 4PM or whatever time you've set as the end of your work day.

End the call as quickly as possible. Now, be prepared because there are some people who simply won't "get it" and you will have to take the same steps a few more times. It's really important that you remain consistent. If you give in you're sending mixed messages. Eventually, family and friends will get the message and stop contacting you during your business hours.

How to Stop Clients From Contacting You After Hours

I think somewhere in the universe there is a rule that says it's okay to call someone any old time because they work from home! In my experience, most clients respect my working hours and make an extra effort to not contact me until the following business day. Unfortunately, this isn't always the case and if you haven't experienced this phenomenon yet... give it time!

Here's the thing...if this is a problem for you now, I'm sorry to break it to you but it's your fault!

What?

Yep.

Just as you should set firm contact rules with your friends and family, you have to do the same with clients. Otherwise you are literally "teaching" them that's it's okay to contact you at any time. You have to let clients know what your contact policy is right from the beginning. This way you will avoid phone calls at 9PM to ask you questions about a project you're working on for them. Or my personal favorite, dropping by on the weekend because they knew you would be home and just wanted to go over some stuff regarding their project or your services. Argh!

Simple Step by Step Plan To Stop Clients From Contacting You After Hours

Step 1

Create a simple SOP (Standard Operating Procedures) manual for new clients. There are several things to include in this and much depends on the nature of your business, but for the purposes of this book on time management, I'll stick with the issues regarding client contact.

Step 2

List your hours of operation unless there is a mutually agreed upon change due to some unforeseen circumstance or emergency. Then list what is considered an emergency.

Include how you wish to be contacted. If by phone, include a contact number and hours. This is really important so that you don't tie up your time talking to clients on the phone unnecessarily. If you're a consultant for example, you may want to set up a system to allow your clients to book appointments on a weekly or monthly basis.

There's a great free booking system for this called BookedIn and you can check that out here:

http://getbookedin.com

You should also include how e-mail correspondence should take place. E-mails going back and forth can be very time consuming. If, however, you don't mind communicating this way, then you may want to stress that the best way to get in touch is via e-mail. State how long it may take to respond so that they're not sitting in front of their PC or staring at their smartphone waiting to hear back from you.

Trust me, this happens more often than you think! So it may be a good idea if it makes sense for your type of business to give an average response time or a simple "I will get back to you as quickly as possible" could be used as well.

If you value your time, don't give clients your personal home or cell numbers. Get a separate phone number for business only. If you're on a tight budget, there are several services available that will allow you to get a virtual local or 800 number for a very small monthly fee. Here are a few that you can check out:

FreedomVoice
http://www.freedomvoice.com

Evoice

http://www.evoice.com

HostedNumbers

http://www.hostednumbers.com

Have your client sign the SOP and make sure you give them a copy. Now in a perfect world every client would read the SOP and abide by it. For the most part, most will respect your time with no problem. But for those who insist on contacting you outside of business hours here's how to handle them.

Scenario- Client keeps calling you even though they know your contact rules.

The first time this happens, gently remind your client about your working hours and suggest that they take a look at the SOP manual for specific details. If your client continues to ignore your hours have a talk with him or her.

Example:

"Your time is valuable and so is mine, so in order to make sure I'm providing you with the best service as well as the best service to my other clients it's important that I maintain consistency when it comes to time. If you need to speak to me about something regarding your account, that's fine. Please call and make an appointment to do so. This way I can give you my undivided attention."

If a client calls after business hours, don't take the call. If they email you outside of whatever rules you've set up, then do not respond. If the client gets upset, calmly remind them what your hours are and that you will gladly get back to them during normal business hours.

This may feel uncomfortable at first, but this really is a normal business expectation. When you have a personal problem with a billing issue, as an example, and you call to complain but instead get a recording that says "Our customer service hours are 9AM to 5PM," you understand that your choice is to either leave a message or call back during business hours. The credit card company doesn't have some guy sitting by the phone just in case someone calls after business hours. You should take the same approach when it comes to your business.

Don't give in. If you give in even one time, you'll have a difficult time getting clients to play by your rules.

How to Manage Distractions Like Facebook & E-mail

It is so easy to lose track of time when you're reading that funny post on your Facebook wall or checking your e-mail for the 10th time in an hour! Phone calls can also eat up your time pretty quickly as well.

You can still engage in all three, but you have to do so with a virtual time clock ticking in your head. We have a built in "I think I'm wasting time" meter. It's just that often we choose to ignore it because whatever we're doing is a lot more fun than working.

Social Network Management

I'm picking on Facebook because most people who are active on Facebook spend a huge amount of time checking messages, chatting with friends, playing games and so on and so on. But the rules would be the same for any social networking site.

If you're on Facebook, Twitter, Foursquare, YouTube and a long list of other sites checking in a lot on your personal account during business hours, you're wasting time. Period. If whatever you're doing isn't focused on business you're also potentially missing out on making money for your business. Have fun on Facebook before or after your business hours.

If you think Facebook time is harmless try this exercise.

The next time you're on Facebook set a timer in another room and go back to your PC. The reason I suggest placing the timer in another room is because it can distract you. I want you to do whatever you normally do on Facebook in the same relaxed manner you're used to doing so. The idea is to get a realistic sample of how much time you spend hanging out on various sites that have nothing to do with work.

Do this every day for a week. Every time you log into Facebook or some other non work-related social networking site, start that timer. When you log out write down the number of minutes you spent on Facebook or other sites. At the end of the week add up all of those minutes.

Then write down on a piece of paper the following sentence:

"This week I spent (insert total number of minutes here during business hours) on Facebook (or other site) writing on my friends walls, looking at photos, videos, timelines etc...instead of doing (insert work related items here)."

Then write down what you could have gotten accomplished in that same amount of time when it comes to your business. Remember, you're only recording the time spent on Facebook during your established working hours. When you force yourself to see things in a tangible way, the impact is a lot stronger and will compel you to pay closer attention to how you're managing your time.

The only other exception to the Facebook rule is if you have a business page that requires you to manage and update frequently. However, even in this instance you should allot a specific amount of time for managing your business page. See the earlier section on strategies for time management for a simple way to create a daily business calendar to help you manage key areas of your business so that you don't waste time.

E-mail

I am guilty of getting sucked into checking e-mail constantly. Although the techniques I'm about to share with you have significantly reduced my addiction to checking my e-mail all the time, I admit it can still be a struggle.

For every business, but especially entrepreneurs working from home, e-mail is almost as important as having a mobile phone. Many times clients and potential new clients contact you almost entirely by e-mail. So there's no way you can avoid not checking your inbox. When you're first starting out, you will find yourself checking e-mail dozens of times a day. You might be waiting for that first e-mail from a new client you're prospecting or an order for your product or service.

If this sounds familiar, you have to focus your time on more important areas of your business. Instead of checking your e-mail and hoping you get that order, focus your time on marketing and networking for business instead.

Create Your Own E-mail SOP

I talked about creating a Standard Operating Procedure for clients and you should create one for yourself as well. In terms of e-mail, create a routine of checking your e-mail at specific times throughout your work day.

Here's an example:

As the first thing at the start of your work day, give yourself a specific amount of time to read and send e-mails. So for instance, you may decide that 30 minutes is enough time. If you have to send a client proposal by e-mail, make sure you've scheduled time to complete the proposal before you sit down to send the e-mail. This way all you have to do is write a quick note, attach the proposal and hit send.

Done!

Then schedule additional times to check e-mail. Maybe right after lunch and again about an hour before you end your work day.

Also make sure you're checking only work related e-mail. This way you will be more likely to stay focused on getting more done than sending an e-mail to your BFF about that cute cat video that went viral! Check personal e-mail during your break time or after work hours.

Avoiding 3 of The Most Common Time Traps

Working from home is something I wouldn't trade for the world! The key to doing so successfully depends a lot on being able to avoid some sneaky common time traps.

Trap #1 – Fun!

Yes you read that correctly. Having fun doing whatever you feel like when you should be working is one of the most difficult things to deal with. Imagine a warm sunny day outside your window and trying to ignore thoughts of going to the beach or the park to goof off for awhile. You wouldn't dream of doing that when you work for someone, or maybe you would but you wouldn't risk losing your job to do so.

When you work from home and have no one to hold you accountable it's a lot easier to convince yourself it's okay to skip work and go have some fun.

A good way to deal with the temptation of fun is to schedule some "fun time" during the week. Pick a time when your schedule permits without sacrificing work-related tasks. In fact, doing it this way can be a great incentive to get projects done earlier than promised. If you can discipline yourself to stay the course the rest of the time, your fun time getaway will be that much sweeter.

Trap # 2 – Television

If you're a reality show junkie or you just like watching television, this activity is a huge time killer. It's so easy to get totally engrossed in an episode of your favorite television program only to then realize that you've spent 2 hours doing nothing but watching TV. It really doesn't matter if it's a soap opera, a crime show or PBS. It's still time wasted.

To combat the urge to watch television, make sure you do not have one in your home office or within close proximity. If your spouse, kids or roommates have televisions ask them to either turn the sound down or watch with headphones. This way you won't be distracted by listening to that fantastic car chase scene!

Trap # 3 – Diet

I cover the subject of your diet and the affects it can have on your ability to focus and think more clearly in a lot more detail in the next section of the book, but I think it's important to touch on it a bit here as well.

Eating calories high in bad carbohydrates like white breads, sugar and flour will not only put weight on you but can also make you sluggish and sleepy. You may also experience "brain fog" where no matter how hard you try, you can't concentrate and get things done in a timely manner.

You can't tell your client that the reason their project isn't complete is because your diet sucks!

Make sure you make it a habit to eat healthier, not just during your business hours, but throughout your entire day. It will make a huge difference in the level of productivity and in your ability to solve problems more effectively.

How To Manage The Amount of Time Spent on Phone Calls

If you're in a service related business, the phone is going to ring and that's a good thing. You just have to have a system in place for managing phone calls in a way that is the most productive for you. Phone conversations can get long and before you know it, you're behind on something you were working on and will have to spend personal time trying to get it done.

Here's how to manage your time when taking business calls.

Clients

Check the caller ID when a call comes in. If it's from a current client and you're expecting their call because they've followed your procedures and made an appointment, you should be prepared in advance.

Jot down a simple agenda.

Here's an example:

Client name
Current project or service
Due dates
Additional information needed to complete the service

Doing this will help you to save time looking for project information when you take the call. Plus it forces you to stay focused. You can also use your agenda to "gently" keep your client focused as well. This may seem a bit much but think of it this way. When someone calls you for any reason, they already have an "agenda" of their own even if they haven't written it down. So don't you think you should have your own agenda as well? Give it a try and see how much more efficient your phone conversations become.

One other technique that I use that can really help you with time management is to decide ahead of time how much time you're going to spend on a phone call. This works best when you have a scheduled phone appointment or conference call.

Unfamiliar Numbers

These could potentially be new clients or telemarketers. If you answer and find it's someone inquiring about your products and services, you can save a lot time by having an "elevator speech" already prepared.

This is a short statement that tells a prospective client who you are and what you do. Also having a website that you can direct them to if they're just collecting information can save you a lot of time by not having to explain everything over the phone. Ask him or her to take a look at your website and if they're interested in your services feel free to make an appointment to discuss their needs further.

Calls From Ads

If you run ads for your business, you can save a lot of time by knowing ahead of time where that person learned about you and your business. By using inexpensive tracking numbers, you will know before you even speak to the person calling, where and how they became aware of you. This way you can avoid wasting time asking where they got your number or which ad they got your number from etc.

Instead you will be able to say something like:

"I ran that ad in the Plumbers Weekly specifically to help plumbers like you to get more business."

If you run ads simultaneously in different mediums and for different clientele, how do you know who's calling about what?

The easy way is by using virtual numbers. Basically you will record a message that only you will hear when you get a call from someone. So for the above example you may record:

"Incoming call from Plumbers Weekly"

Right away you will be prepared to address specific needs because you will know ahead of time where they got your information and why they're calling. Here is that list mentioned in the previous section:

FreedomVoice
http://www.freedomvoice.com

Evoice
http://www.evoice.com

HostedNumbers
http://www.hostednumbers.com

How To Stop Procrastinating

There is no magic trick I can give you to stop putting things off. If you procrastinate every now and then, it's not a big deal. We all do it from time to time. If, on the other hand, you've developed a reputation for never getting things done in a timely manner, you've got work to do.

Mindset

First you have to make up your mind to change. Procrastination is a bad habit you have to break. You can change but only if you're willing to put in the effort.

Creating New Habits

The best approach, in my opinion, is to make changes a little bit at a time. You didn't develop the procrastination habit overnight and you won't change overnight. So make small changes consistently over time.

Find Your Personal Breaking Point

A personal breaking point is when something significant to you has to happen to force you to take action and get something done on time. Everyone has one.

For example, I had a friend who would wait until he got a "cut off" notice before he would pay his electric bill. This guy had the money to pay, but he just refused to take care of it for whatever reason. One day he forgot to pay and he arrived home to find his home in total darkness! By the way, it was in the middle of a traditional snowy Chicago winter!

Cold + Darkness = Personal Breaking Point!

He did not like being in the dark and cold. He never waited until the last minute to pay his electric bill after that.

What Happens If You Don't Get It Done?

Think about what will happen if you don't get something done when it comes to your business. What will be the consequences? This is similar to the statement I gave you earlier except now you're making yourself directly responsible. It's a heavier burden to carry if your inability to get things done results in your family not having the things they need to lead a happier life.

It can be different if the consequences include the well-being of others in your life.

The reason some people never try to change bad habits like procrastination is because they haven't had to deal with the consequences. You can't wait until you experience a consequence of not doing something. That could mean the end of your business.

Start Small

Focus on changing your habits by starting with smaller things first. Procrastinators don't just put off things that relate to just one area of their lives. So start with the little things first and build up to bigger and bigger things. If you stay committed to change and stay consistent, you will conquer procrastination and enjoy a lot more success in many areas of your life.

Use Diet & Exercise to Help You Focus Better & Get More Done

How Diet And Exercise Can Help You Focus And Get More Done

In this section you're going to learn the importance of diet and exercise when you work from home. Certain foods can actually give you energy and help clear away the cobwebs when you're trying to focus. You'll also learn which foods can help you be more creative and keep extra pounds from creeping up.

Really? Food Can Help Me Manage My Time Better?

When you eat a diet rich in foods that actually feed your brain, you will begin to notice changes in your ability to focus which means the quality of your work will be better.

Certain foods also elevate your mood, which means you're more likely to work with a positive attitude. That can make a big difference in how you approach even the toughest parts of your business.

There are other ways to revive your tired brain so that you can work more efficiently. This includes regular exercise and additional strategies that can give you the added benefit of taking little work breaks throughout your busy day.

Let's get started!

Simple Ways To Enjoy Better Mental Focus

No matter what type of business you're in, it's so important to take regular mind breaks throughout your day. Your brain gets tired and mental fatigue sets in if you don't take a break.

When you're mentally tired you're literally operating on fumes just trying to finish whatever you're working on. That's also when critical mistakes happen. You may have heard about the German bank employee who fell asleep on his keyboard and accidentally transferred $293 million dollars into an account. The original amount was the equivalent of about $55.00! Ouch!

See what can happen? Imagine if you made certain mistakes in your business. How much time and money could you end up losing?

3 Ways To Stay Mentally Fresh

1. Get plenty of sleep
This doesn't mean that you have to sleep 8 hours a night. Everyone is different and not everyone needs 8 hours. You know better than anyone how much sleep you need in order to function at your best each day. If you're not getting enough sleep due to insomnia, check with your doctor to rule out anything health related. If everything checks out okay with your health, check to see if your nightly routine may be keeping you awake at night. Too much television or caffeine, for example, may be interfering with your sleep patterns.

2. Eat "Happy Carbs!"
I like to refer to certain foods as happy carbs because they don't put you on the emotional roller-coaster ride you get from high sugar foods like soft drinks, cookies, cake etc. Instead go for fruits with a low level of sugar.

Oranges, cherries, grapefruit, apples and grapes are all great choices and will satisfy your sweet tooth. Although they all contain sugar, the fiber in the fruit slows down the absorption of the sugar in your body. So stock up!

3. Eat Protein

Protein produces an amino acid called tryptophan. It is one of the amino acids needed by neurotransmitters to send vital messages to our brains. Unfortunately, our bodies cannot manufacture tryptophan and we must get it from the foods we eat. Soy, lean meat, eggs and dairy are all great sources of protein and aid in getting our neurotransmitters the tryptophan they need. The result is a perkier brain which allows you to get tasks done and maintain greater focus throughout the day.

How To Get More Energy Throughout Your Day

When you work for yourself it requires a lot more energy to get everything done. You're juggling a lot and often under more pressure to bring home the bacon! If your energy isn't up to par, your ability to be productive and get things done on schedule can suffer quite a bit. In this section you'll learn which foods are both healthy and natural energy boosters. Plus you'll learn some other strategies for maintaining energy throughout the work day!

Here is a list of foods that can lift your energy levels and help with productivity!

Energy Boosting Foods

Figs
They taste delicious and are natural energy boosters. You can get the same energizing benefits from both natural and dried figs.

Raisins
Snack on these to jump start your energy levels and they're also natural antioxidants.

Sunflower Seeds
When you're feeling fatigued, snack on some sunflower seeds to give you some much needed energy.

Watermelon
Not only does it taste good but it's good for you! Watermelon is loaded with nutrients and is very low in calories. It's also a known energy booster.

Water
Drink lots of water throughout the day and not only will you have more energy, water helps to cleanse your body of toxins. So drink up! Aim for 8 glasses a day.

Brain Food to Snack On

Almonds
Like most nuts, almonds are loaded with Vitamin E. That makes them great for improving skin, hair and brain power!

Walnuts
Rich in Omega-3 fatty acids, these nuts help you to think clearly and that means less time wasted.

Non-Food Ways to Boost Energy and Your Ability to Think More Clearly

Take a Power Nap
Assuming you are getting enough sleep at night, you might be able receive some real benefit from taking a 20-30 minute nap during your day. The freedom to implement this strategy is one of the great benefits of working from home. You do want to be careful though if you are someone who, instead of a quick power nap, ends up sleeping for hours at a time. This could leave you feeling groggy and less inclined to want to head back into your work routine. Your goal is to feel refreshed and ready to work again!

Take a Short Walk
When you feel your energy waning during the work day, sometimes a brisk walk outside can do wonders. Getting your heart rate up a bit while enjoying the fresh air can have a great impact on clearing your mind and getting your energy level up again.

Meditation
You don't have to be a guru to get the wonderful benefits of meditation. Lots of research has been done on the effects meditation has on the mind and body. Those who meditate daily tend to be able to handle stress better and think more clearly.

Prayer

Many people who engage in prayer daily say that they feel more confident, peaceful and a lot more optimistic, all of which can help to propel your business through the roof!

Visualization Exercises

Athletes like Pro basketball players are taught to visualize every aspect of the game before they play. They hear the crowd in their mind, feel the excitement and energy and see the ball going into the net. Taking a few minutes each morning to visualize the outcome of your day can be a great way to boost your energy and your confidence.

Deep Breathing

When you're feeling mentally drained stop and take 5 slow deep breaths. This will help your body to release tension and provide you with more energy and focus.

3 Ways To Avoid The Dreaded "Work From Home 10"

Ever heard of the "Freshmen 10?" It's the average amount of weight you supposedly gain your first year in college. If you live in the dorms, 3 square meals come with the territory and man do they feed you well! Lots of high starchy foods and sugary treats. Of course there are healthier options but the not so healthy food is also available in abundance. Plus there's a pizza place on almost every corner!

When you begin working from home, it's really easy to get so focused on work and growing your business that exercise just isn't part of the plan. This is especially true if you've never been the type to work out on a regular basis.

When you work for an employer, usually it means commuting to work either by car or public transportation. You may take the stairs and, depending on where you work, you may have a good walk to the office from the parking lot. That's not exactly getting quality exercise but it is certainly better than nothing.

Unless you have an exercise routine in place, working from home can mean your daily commute is 40 feet from your bedroom. It can also mean you spend an extended amount of time just sitting. At least in an office environment you may have to deliver documents, attend meetings and such that allows you to get some form of exercise.

If you're not eating a healthy diet and sitting around for several hours, the pounds can creep up on you before you know it.

Here are some ways to avoid gaining weight while you work from home.

#1 - Plan Your Meals Ahead of Time
One of the best ways to insure that you will be grabbing a lunch and snacks that are healthy during your busy work day, is to be prepared ahead of time. This means allowing time to plan your meals and shop for the groceries that you will need to have on hand.

Prepping healthy veggies and having a good selection of fruit and other healthy snacks ready to go, can really help you to make better choices when you are very busy. Preparation is key when it comes to your healthy diet.

#2 - Get Moving!

Take 30 minutes each day and schedule exercise. You could go for a brisk walk, get on a treadmill, ride a bike, do Yoga, Tai Chi or even lift weights. The key is to just get moving to get your heart pumping and give your muscles a work out.

The benefits in terms of health can be dramatic over time, plus you can lose weight if you need to and avoid putting on extra pounds.

#3 - Stand Up!

Instead of taking phone calls sitting down, stand up and walk around. Even when you're not on the phone, try working while standing. Try taking 5 minute breaks and get up from your desk and walk around your home office. Do some stretching exercises. You can even run or walk in place for a few minutes.

#4 - Get A Trainer

Investing in a personal trainer is a great way to stay in shape. He or she can keep you on track with diet choices and design a workout regimen that will allow you to get fit. It can be really good to have someone else keep you accountable when it comes to diet and exercise.

Exercise Can Help Keep You From Getting Depressed

Going out on your own to work for yourself can be risky and scary for some. Not having a regular paycheck to depend on can cause stress and turn you into an emotional wreck. Next thing you know, you'll find yourself getting way behind on client projects or marketing for new clients because you're feeling emotionally unwell.

A regular exercise routine will keep the blues away because when you exercise your body releases endorphins that make you feel good. When you're feeling good you make better decisions, get more done and are less likely to waste time.

How To Schedule Exercise Into Your Work Day

30 Minutes Is All It Takes!

The most common excuse for not working out is not having enough time to get it done. That's not a reason, it's an excuse. Getting exercise is a must, especially when you work from home.

Unlike people who work outside of the home, your commute is measured in feet and not miles. No long walks from the parking lot to get a bit of exercise. So you're going to have to make time to get it done. Think of it this way, if you're the only one running your business and you don't have a back-up plan, you owe it to yourself and your family to make sure you're getting exercise to increase your chances of staying healthy.

How To Get It Done

A minimum of 30 minutes of exercise each day is the recommended amount to become more fit. In the beginning, try different times of the day to see what feels best for you. If you're a morning person, try scheduling your 30 minutes first thing each morning. You can also work out after quitting time. That's a great way to unwind from the day and clear your head.

Breaks

Schedule a 30 minute break during your work hours to go for a walk. Not only will you feel better, but walking is a great way to spark new ideas and come up with solutions to problems you may be working on. Walking puts you in a naturally relaxed state of mind and allows you to think better. If you can't do 30 minutes, then schedule two 15 minute breaks at different times during your day. You'll still get all the benefits.

Exercise To-Do List

Add exercise to your daily to-do list. When you write it down and make it as important as sending a proposal to a client, you're reinforcing the importance of getting your exercise in each day.

Write it down and really commit to actually following through. If that's not enough to get you to exercise try this.

Write down the consequences of not getting regular exercise and place it where you can see it every day.

Who will provide for your family if your diet and lack of exercise causes a major illness?

If you have children, how will your choices affect their lives?

What if you lose the business you worked so hard to build because you can't work every day?

When you put down what you may lose if you don't take better care of yourself, it can be all the motivation you need to get up and get moving!

Time Management for Work from Home Parents

The Challenge for Parents

Trying to run a business from home with children is tough. After all, raising children is a full-time job too. Although I'm not a parent, I have several friends who work from home and have kids, so for this section of the book I decided to tap their brains a bit to find out how they manage their work time and family time.

The tips and strategies are not in any particular order. I suggest that you read each one and take what works for you in your current situation. What you might find is that even if a particular tip does not address your problem specifically, it may spark some ideas on how to work from home and still enjoy the love and fun of your children.

Tips for Balancing Parenting and Your Business

Many parents run successful businesses out of their homes while also raising happy and healthy children. You can do this too and use the flexibility of having your own schedule to your advantage. It just takes some organization and prioritizing from the beginning to make it work.

How to Get Work Done When You Have Young Children At Home

If you have children who are in school, you'll have to schedule your office hours to coincide with their school hours. That's a no brainer but you should also create an additional "family to-do list" alongside your business to-do list. This way your "work" never interferes with your family time. With so much to get done running your business it's easy to forget that soccer game you promised to attend.

If, on the other hand, you have toddlers at home you've got to have a completely different game plan. Consider hiring a babysitter to watch your kids during working hours. It's not a perfect solution but can go a long way towards giving you the time you need to get your work done.

Toddlers require a lot of attention that you won't be able to give while speaking with a client on the phone. Hiring a babysitter to watch your child can relieve you of a lot of stress and limit the amount of distractions you face while you work.

Schedules

If you have to pick up your kids from school each day, you should add this to your daily schedule. Even though it's a daily event, you should put it on your to-do list because you'll find it easier to schedule work projects around this time during the day. You won't feel stressed out because you have to stop working on something to pick up the kids. You will instead work more efficiently because that time of day is a regular scheduled event, just as writing that new book, working on promotional activities or making phone calls are a part of your regular working day.

What's most important is that you make sure the time you schedule to pick up your kids includes spending time with them. Talk to them about their day and help them with their homework. Decide how much time to allot. It could be an hour, it could be 2 hours. That's up to you. Whatever you decide, make sure that you are always consistent. Kids need consistency, especially from you. It also lets them know that they are a priority in your life.

Outsourcing

In the earlier part of the book on strategies for time management, I included a section on leveraging your time by outsourcing certain tasks. Work from home parents can benefit immensely by hiring virtual assistants. Instead of trying to do everything on your own, you can outsource administrative tasks like bookkeeping, writing business proposals, maintaining updates on your website, graphics and much more. It all depends on how much of your business you feel comfortable handing off to someone else.

Delegating tasks to someone you've hired frees up more of your time to work on client projects, get more business and most importantly to spend more time with your kids. After all, if you're working sun up to sun down, the negative effects on your children can last a lifetime.

Helping Children To Understand That You Are Working

This can be tough especially if you have toddlers. All they know or care about is that Mommy or Daddy is home and available for whatever they need. They don't care about work and don't understand what that means.

You may have to consider working around your toddler's schedule. That may mean getting up very early and working on the most demanding task while they are still asleep. It may be difficult to take calls or place calls with a toddler running around. You could try making calls and answering e-mails during nap time or while your toddler is being entertained by something on television, preferably something fun but also educational.

It's not impossible to run a business when you have very young toddlers in the home, but it will be very challenging. You may have to work on projects later in the evening once your little ones are fast asleep.

Establishing Work Routines For Children

It's a lot easier to teach older children certain rules when you're working from home. Let your children see where you work and explain to them what you do. Answer their questions and allow them to learn as much as they would like to about your work.

Children are proud of their parents and it makes them feel a lot more confident when another child or adult asks them what their parent does for work.

When you let them into your working world they will be more likely to respect the rules about not disturbing you while you are working.

For example:

Instead of telling your kids not to bother you because you're working, tell them you will be working with some really important clients between 3:00PM and 4:00PM or whatever time you decide. Then ask your kids to make a really cool sign that you can hang on the outside of your office door to remind them you're working with clients. They'll get a kick out of making that sign and at the same time they will associate something positive with your work events.

End of The Work Day

Always end your work schedule at the same time each day. Children need to spend time with you and will eagerly anticipate getting to hang out with you. It also shows them that while your work is important, it's not more important than spending time with them. Always be sure to schedule time with your kids and spouse after your work day. Don't go watch television and complain about being too tired to spend time with your kids. Otherwise they will grow to resent your work and may feel they aren't worth your time.

Work Free Weekends

It's really important to maintain focus and get work done during the week. That may mean a late night or two after your kids are asleep. Manage your work time using some of the techniques in this book so that you're not working when you should be spending time with your family. Let the weekends be for family time only. That means no e-mail, no client calls and no work meetings.

You may be a work from home mom or dad but your most important job is being a parent. So never let your business become more important than your children...no exceptions!

Virtual Business & Your Mobile Office

Virtual Business & Your Mobile Office

One of the most amazing things that I've personally experienced as a result of having my own business has been the ability to be completely location independent. Of course this will not be a goal for everyone reading this book, but if the idea of travel or picking up and moving whenever the mood strikes you is appealing, then this section is for you.

If being location independent is one of your main goals in having your own business, you'll obviously need to create a business model that will work for you regardless of where you are physically located. This means that service type businesses that involve location dependent or face-to-face meetings with clients are not going to be the best fit for you.

Certainly there are plenty of service related businesses that can work virtually and, depending on your current skills and interests, could be a great fit for the person who does not want to stay in one place for great lengths of time. Here are some examples: web design, graphic design, SEO, social media management, ghost writing, customer service, virtual coaching and the list goes on.

And if you are in a position to be working 100% for yourself and not be working with clients, you could create niche websites or my favorite recommendation to anyone with a desire to write would be to become a self published author. I consider a writer to be in the best position of all when it comes to taking your work with you anywhere in the world. I can say this from experience as I sit writing this book from an island in Thailand. I made the leap myself and every moment of the freedom I feel has been so worth it.

To begin with, even if you are not quite ready to make that leap to move out of your home or to another country, start thinking about your tech gear and day-to-day business and what it would mean to pack that up to take on the go with you.

Firstly, this will cut down a lot on the amount of physical things that you buy for your business and personal use. You probably want to be able to travel as lightly as possible.

Before I left for Thailand, I had found the perfect computer backpack and this became my "virtual office" while I was still living in the U.S. I made sure it contained everything I'd need for a day out working from Starbucks or various other cafes. I learned exactly what I could eliminate and the types of items I might need to consider adding to my mobile office space.

You'll need to think about things like battery life and power adapters, depending on where you are planning to go and for how long you will typically be without a power source.

You also have many options these days regarding communication online, so even if you are outside of your home country, you can easily keep in touch with family, friends and clients. Skype is a great free tool that can be used for real time instant message, chat or video. There are also additional paid for services that are not very expensive. For example, you can purchase a phone number that people can use to call you without having to dial via another country code. This means that the caller will not incur additional charges and you are able to pick up the call or message via your Skype account.

You can get a free account for Skype here: http://www.skype.com

Only you know what types of gear will be essential for your business as you think about making a big move like this. Begin thinking about it early and enjoy the planning phase and reaching this milestone if it's a dream of yours.

Final Word - It's Up To You Now

I hope that you've found the strategies I've shared with you useful and easy to follow. There's one more thing I want to mention to you. Don't beat yourself up if you don't get your time management skills in order overnight.

Although most of the strategies revealed here were designed to take effect quickly, you may find yourself skipping a day or two. No matter how simple or great the strategies might be, managing time is a new habit you have to build upon.

It all starts with a willingness to change. Once you decide to move forward, you'll be excited and more confident in every area of your life, not just your business.

You can read every strategy over and over again but you have to put them into practice to enjoy the benefits each can provide.

If you've enjoyed this book, I'd really appreciate it if you would take a moment to leave an honest review. I'd really love to hear from you, and I very much appreciate your comments as I love to put a name to those who are serious about creating change in their lives.

Also, I'm a big believer that knowledge is power so I suggest that you take a look at the recommendations that I've listed in the next section of the book. These are additional resources that I believe will help you with your own productivity and I want you to have the biggest list of ideas and strategies available to you so that you can pick and choose which will work for you.

Good luck and I wish you the very best success in business and in life!

Jessica

http://www.amazon.com/author/jessicamarks

Recommended Reads

HBR Guide to Getting the Right Work Done (Harvard Business Review)
http://www.amazon.com/dp/B009G1SUDS/

The Myths of Innovation
http://www.amazon.com/dp/B0026OR2PE/

Getting Things Done: The Art of Stress-Free Productivity
http://www.amazon.com/dp/B000WH7PKY/

18 Minutes: Find Your Focus, Master Distraction, and Get the Right Things Done
http://www.amazon.com/dp/B004QZ9POM/

Becoming The 1%: How To Master Productivity And Rise To The Top In 7 Days
http://www.amazon.com/dp/B00AAESF3U/

The Checklist Manifesto: How to Get Things Right
http://www.amazon.com/dp/B0030V0PEW/

Master Getting Things Done the David Allen Way with Evernote: Your 7-Day GTD Immediate Action Plan
http://www.amazon.com/dp/B00CXTDQES/

The 4-Hour Work Week: Escape the 9-5, Live Anywhere and Join the New Rich
http://www.amazon.com/dp/B006X0M2TS/

What the Most Successful People Do Before Breakfast: A Short Guide to Making Over Your Mornings--and Life
http://www.amazon.com/dp/B007K3E2YK/

Eat That Frog!: 21 Great Ways to Stop Procrastinating and Get More Done in Less Time
http://www.amazon.com/dp/B001AFF25W/

www.ingramcontent.com/pod-product-compliance
Lightning Source LLC
Chambersburg PA
CBHW060616200326
41521CB00007B/782